BlackBerry® Fool

BlackBerry®Fool

An addict's guide to switching off

CAPSTONE

Contents

Introduction

Unless you have been living under a stone or in the deepest parts of the Amazon jungle over the last few years, it is likely that you have heard of the BlackBerry®*. It's even possible that you're using one right now, to read this book, in which case it'll be interesting to see how long you can hold your attenti...

... new voicemail about the sales numbers...I wonder if anyone's replied to my funny email with the YouTube video, the one with the cat falling into the custard... I see Bob's put some photos of his new patio on Facebook...

...and you're back in the room.

Ask any of the 21 million executives who currently use a BlackBerry and they will tell you how wonderful it is; how they can't live without it; that it is now possible to be in the office without having to be *in* the office. What they won't tell you is that having a BlackBerry means no longer ever really *leaving* the office either.

●

There is no doubt that the BlackBerry is a godsend to the modern professional, especially those modern professionals who don't like face-to-face communication. It is also great for those who need to be ever present and ever engaged with the workplace: to be on demand and in demand 24x7. Some say the ego enhancing experience is better than sex.

As useful as your BlackBerry may seem, there is also a dark side and it's not a sexy dark side either – not like Darth Vader's, the one he uses to zap enemies and peel grapes. No, the BlackBerry also has a *dork* side, one that controls the destiny of every executive who crosses over to it: just ask their long suffering family, secretary, friends and local parish priest. Hence why in some quarters (mainly those people who don't use one) the BlackBerry is euphemistically known as the *Crackberry*; let the force be with you.

•

Every piece of technology has its drawbacks. Just as PowerPoint can help transmit ideas but more often than not just destroys the art of working a crowd, so the BlackBerry can ruin business and personal relationships. It does so by fusing the business and the personal together into a single high-pressure stream.

But perhaps the BlackBerry isn't really a technological problem at all. Perhaps it's about us. Give us a great tool like the BlackBerry and we'll use it for everything. But beware the adage *a fool with a tool is still a fool*: if you give a fool a tool the result will merely be more foolishness. The BlackBerry is very good at making even the most suave of us look socially inept and clumsy. Fondle it all day and you'll appear comical and a tiny bit sad all at once, two things we'll remind you of throughout this book.

●

So this book is not about the BlackBerry per se, it's about you and getting some of your life back. After reading it, no-one expects you'll stuff your BlackBerry in the bin or under the wheel of a bus and revert to the quill pen. And, you'll be glad to know, neither will your partner or your kids. You will, however, feel a little more in control and a little more liberated from the vibrating gizmo that directs your every waking hour. Who knows, you may even fall in love with it again. You might feel that warm glow of satisfaction each time you caress its tiny screen. In a tender moment together, perhaps you'll even clean out the food smeared over the keys that day you dropped it in the anniversary dinner, the same dinner your wife booked because you're still getting round to keying anniversaries in your BlackBerry calendar.

If you no longer want to be considered a *Blackberry Fool* or to be in a *Blackberry Jam* or to be observed *Blackberry Picking*, then read on. This book is more effective than self-hypnosis, less painful than repetitive strain injury and cheaper than a divorce.

Blackberry Picking

Blackberry Picking is the name given to the obsessive checking of one's BlackBerry for new emails.

●

BlackBerries display unread messages in **bold font**. It's not to help users prioritise new messages over old. It's to stimulate the same kind of mania induced by popping bubble wrap. Clicking on fresh emails and popping bubble wrap both produce an overwhelming (and illusory) sense of progress. It's powerful too – stare at a screen of *somebody else's* unread emails and you'll soon feel a rising urge to start clicking. Congratulations – you're *Blackberry Picking*.

●

It matters not whether the email is from the boss, a colleague or E-Z Viagra Inc. A Blackberry Picker is undiscerning. Any email will be enough to grab the attention. The high doesn't last, of course, and you're soon interrogating the palms of your hands for a new fix, for evidence that somebody out there is thinking of you.

People themselves never knew they had them."

Agatha Christie (1890 – 1976)

Stop treating life as a quest to attain a zero inbox

Tip 1

If scientists can't reach absolute zero then it is highly unlikely that you will do the same with your inbox. Even if you did, it pays to think about what might happen as a result. Firstly, your colleagues will suspect you of deleting the lot, like a postman who dumps his mailbags in a ditch when he can't stand it any more. Secondly, you will receive more emails, sure as you're born. And with no other emails to deal with, the next message to arrive at your pristine inbox will stand out in your mind like God's final message to creation, even if it's only an email from reception letting someone know they've left their headlights on. It's likely you will become irrationally occupied by headlights, wandering from desk to desk asking about registration plate AXO4 FHU like it's a spectacle. Whatever happens, you won't start doing any of the things you promised you'd do once you finished all your mails.

So what should you do now you see that a zero inbox is a pipe dream? Well at appropriate times, simply check your email and respond to what needs a response and accept that there will always be another email. Only losers and loafing postmen boast about having a zero inbox.

Don't be on call all the time

Very few of us have a job where we need to be available all the time. Does your job involve nuclear stuff? No? Then you don't need to be on call all the time. Go home.

Of course technology *allows* us to be always on call, but that doesn't mean we need to be. In fact, you'll soon notice that always being on call simply becomes the new expectation. The more extended our window of working, the more is expected of us, like a modern day Sisyphus, the Greek god cursed for all eternity to roll a giant builder up a hill only to watch it roll back down again. His crime? The other gods caught him spreading racy gossip and claiming to be smarter than everyone else, two classic hallmarks of the BlackBerry user if ever there were. Sisyphus didn't actually have a BlackBerry, but he sounds like he'd have been an early adopter.

Don't take it with you

Simply because the BlackBerry can be with you at all times doesn't mean it must be. Practise leaving it at work when going home and at home when going out. You are not obliged to drag it around with you like some comfy blanket. Decide on its default home and stick to it, perhaps your desk, or your kitchen drawer – not your handbag, your shirt pocket or wedged into your crash helmet. Under no circumstances should you bring your BlackBerry into private spots, such as the toilet. One does occasionally see a chap standing at a urinal and blithely chatting away into their BlackBerry. It's hard to work out whether the person on the other end is so important that their call must be taken *no matter what*, or so unimportant that they're worth calling only when peeing.

And having both hands free is no excuse, ladies.

Recognise that BlackBerry use is addictive

Scientists can train a rat to feed itself by pressing a lever which dispenses a peanut. Suddenly the rat can eat whenever it likes. From an evolutionary point of view, it really doesn't stand a chance: it soon becomes totally addicted to pressing the lever. Even if the scientists stop dispensing the peanut, our rat will carry on pressing the lever *for days*. It's not a biological addiction – levers have no biological significance to a rat – but it shows that a BlackBerry addiction needn't have a biological basis. You can see addictive technology everywhere. Witness gambling on slot-machines. The gambler gets just enough reward to keep going. Bells ring, lights flash and occasionally a fraction of the money paid in is spat out, to great fanfare. It feels good: it feels like your coin caused the whistles and bells to happen. It feels like you're playing the machine, when of course it's the machine that's playing you. Just as the rat and the gambler presses the lever looking for a payout, the BlackBerry user is conditioned to look in their inbox for a funny joke or a bit of idle gossip. If you don't accept that's what's happening, you might condem yourself to glimpsing your entire life through a screen, darkly.

Beware the idiot lantern

There are certain places, such as a darkened cinema, where the glow of the BlackBerry screen will make the Blackberry Picker appear to be silly, ghostly and poor company all at once. Recall that the television set, which was the must-have whizz-bang gadget of the 1950s, was often referred to as 'The Idiot Lantern', even back then. It was never clear whether the phrase referred to a lantern stared at by idiots, or a lantern which helps us to spot idiots in the dark, the better to avoid sitting next to one. Both definitions could have been crafted for the Blackberry Picker, lighting himself up like a Christmas tree two minutes before the movie starts. The beam of the idiot lantern also shines brightly in hospital waiting rooms, shining upon those Blackberry Pickers sitting directly underneath the sign asking to switch off phone or risk interfering with medical equipment. Think about what the Blackberry Picker is saying to us at that point: that if they have to choose between relaxing or causing the X-ray machine operator to emit blue smoke, blue smoke wins every time.

Blackberry Fool

A *Blackberry Fool* is someone who thinks their device makes them look more important, impressive and productive. Naturally the *Fool* is wrong on every count. They can't keep their inbox empty and they fail to impress anyone. These days, being contactable 24x7 is really not the fashionable thing, not when the rich and famous are unreachable and answer to no-one.

●

Richard Branson gets up when he wants. If he's never late for an event it's because the event starts only when he arrives. *That's* time management. Right now, Rupert Murdoch might be on his yacht, in the air or talking to the Russian prime minister in Moscow Square. No-one knows, and *that's* cool. Possessing Barak Obama's direct dial number will get you arrested, and *that's* impressive.

●

Incommunicado is the new luxury. It's an exclusive club that doesn't admit *Blackberry Fools*.

"It is far more impressive when others discover your good qualities without your help."

Judith Martin, *Miss Manners* columnist

Enjoy the moment

Take time out to rediscover the things that would grab your attention as a child or a teenager; a sunset, a perfect afternoon in the garden. Enjoy the conversation, the film, the train journey, the walk to the deli. If you are always on your BlackBerry you won't actually get to enjoy much at all and you may become inured to the good, free things around you. Why constantly worry about what's in your inbox? You'll probably always have one: it will probably always be full – what's the rush? Be present to what's present. A great conversation with your children can never, ever be repeated, and when they are older they may be less willing to talk (perhaps they'll email you instead – poetic justice!). Life is uncertain: none of us know the minute or the hour that our number is up, so be here now and enjoy the journey.

Sentence yourself to hard labour

Tip 2

We all need some balance and variety in our work, whether we are a manual worker or a knowledge worker. For knowledge workers, a little manual labour is critical. Your brain is only 4% of your body mass. If you use your head all day then you risk burning out mentally and physically – a far more common problem than people admit, one that manual labour can help prevent. When was the last time you did any of the following?

- gardening
- dancing
- walking and hiking
- weights at the gym
- led the final rebel assault on the Death Star
  (with the kids, in the garden)

If you're an office worker, don't be fooled into thinking that you can improve productivity merely by thinking harder. If you've ever said to yourself, 'Come on brain, hurry up – think!', then you're not alone: it's a technique also used by Homer Simpson. Go ahead and copy him, if you see yourself as a loveable moron living a life worthy of a slapstick cartoon. For the rest of us the moral of the story is that there is no such thing as hurry up thinking. Your brain doesn't have an accelerator pedal. Slow down to the speed of your thought. Any faster and you'll be driving with the handbrake on.

Too much work makes Jack a dull boy

Tip 3

A BlackBerry might make the *Fool* feel like a corporate superhero, but you know better. You know that a BlackBerry is largely a device for piping other people's to-do lists directly into your lap. If you build your daily agenda around your inbox then your day becomes no more than the sum of all the tasks other people have set for you. You'll find it hard to find the time to do what you enjoy, or learn new skills, or even to do your actual job. This is why fencing off our email is so important: we need to zone it into part of our day, not have it course throughout the day and at home at night as well. Really put your heart and soul into zoning your time. Think about 8/8/8.

> 8 hours work
> 8 hours play
> 8 hours sleep

Doesn't that sound good? It's far better than 18 hours work and six hours sleep. And remember all work and no play makes Jack a friendless workaholic. The faster you respond to everyone's emails the sooner you'll condition your co-workers into expecting a quick turnaround from you. Answer on a Sunday afternoon and they'll expect that of you for ever more.

Are you working *hard* or just working *looong*?

Tip 4 Search Google for Seth Godin's brilliant essay, '*Labor Day*', in which he writes of the difference between working *long* and working *hard*. Everyone likes to think that they work hard, but what does hard work mean these days? It used to mean long hours and dangerous, dirty working conditions, like our great grandparents experienced. These days, working hard means something very different. What our generation considers hard work is really just working *long* hours for big companies. Don't think you work hard simply because you're thumbing the BlackBerry late into the night from your home or the airport – you're just working *long*, and maybe losing out to more adventurous souls working *hard*. Hard work means staying sharp and taking risks. In a time of rapid change, it means never getting too comfortable in your job title or your industry, It might even mean quitting your job, which in turn means dealing with the risk of failure in your next venture. It's hard work to risk failure, to constantly seek new challenges and ways of working. Godin points out that Sam Walton, billionaire founder of Wal-Mart, didn't work longer hours than many corporate folk do now. Instead, Walton worked *hard*: he started with next to nothing, took risks and he constantly experimented.

Don't measure your self-worth by your workload

Tip 5 At some point in the last century a great cult of busyness sprang up. It isn't an easily recognisable cult – there's no big mansion, kooky ceremonies or emptied bank accounts – but there's no doubt it's a cult and sad to say, it has many disciples, and like every cult it also has some strange beliefs. Somewhere along the line, it became commendable for a person to appear maxed out: it became cool to have more work on than one could possibly handle. Cults often end in tears. The cult of busyness should end with the realisation that the commercial world is all about perpetual growth and expansion. There is literally no end to it. Email is continuously mushrooming. There will always be more email. Faced with a task master that never sleeps, you need to create your own punctuation points, a time when you forget the sales figures for a while, when you say the email will manage without you. It's easier to achieve if you measure your self-esteem not by your diary but by your goals, your results, your values and the company you keep. Give it a go. If it doesn't work, you can always go back to wearing a funny robe and chanting that you've got back-to-back meetings all week.

Blackberry W(h)ine

The Blackberry Whine is the cry of anguish from a *Blackberry Fool* who becomes cut off from their email. *Blackberry Whiners* can be heard to howl from a distance, especially in habitats with no wi-fi reception and high roaming charges. Bereft of their electronic guide, mentor, motivator and true friend, the *Whiner* just isn't sure how to handle all the free time available. Some begin to melt right there on the spot, just as surely as if you'd thrown a bucket of water over The Wicked Witch of the West or opened the Ark of the Covenant without saying the correct mumbo-jumbo first.

●

And even if you're not sure how *you* came to be falling to pieces simply because you can't look up those two film references on YouTube because the wi-fi is down, please know there is a way out.

" Think not about your frustrations,
but about your unfulfilled potential.
Concern yourself not with what you
tried and failed in, but with what it is
still possible for you to do."

Pope John XXIII

React however you will, then *think* about your reaction

Tip 1
This gets easier once you realise that everyone has two kinds of brain. One kind served our ancestors well – running away from sabre tooth tigers, running toward Raquel Welch dressed as a cavewoman, that sort of thing – and then there's the second kind of brain, the modern day kind of brain that can answer obscure questions on TV quiz shows. Your caveman brain deals with automatic behaviours and emotions – see tiger, RUN! – while your *'Who Wants To Be A Millionaire'* brain handles all your reasoning. When faced with what we think is a life-threatening emergency, our older brain takes over and our reasoning brain takes a back seat. The older brain has fewer weapons in its armoury, and most of them involve adrenalin. And just in case you hadn't realised, being unable to access your emails is not an emergency. No adrenalin required, thank you. Be resourceful, cut the melodrama, have a coffee, smell the flowers. Above all, realise that swearing and shouting won't change anything.

Don't panic

Panic is a popular reaction to life's little setbacks, partly because it feels better than sitting there doing nothing and laughing at the wonder of it all, even though it rarely is. There'd be less panic if we wised up to our true nature, our highly acquisitive nature. As human beings we can't help having a materialistic bent, especially when it comes to useful little tools like the BlackBerry. Give us a BlackBerry and a good signal and we're happy: take that trinket away and we panic. Again, it all goes back to caveman days – our ancestors had to fight literally tooth and nail just to get a meal, so we've evolved a very strong sense of scarcity. It rises up whenever we lose something. But when you 'lose' your connection to email, are you really losing anything? Your state has changed, sure, but what have you *lost*? You will get your emails back at some point in the very near future. If you can't log on right now, why not declare it to be a 'magic moment' and use the time to think about the bigger picture of your business or life, or take the time to go do something you've never done before.

Use your intelligence

You have three forms of intelligence; neural, experiential and reflective, and they each differ in their ability to withstand life's hustle and bustle. Neural intelligence is genetic, so you're kind of stuck with that. Experiential intelligence comes from having been around a bit, having done things a few times before and learning from your mistakes. Reflective intelligence is the fragile one, the one that goes out the window when we're busy. Reflective intelligence makes you stop and think, 'Hey, maybe there's a different or even better way of doing things than relying wholly on my BlackBerry? Maybe my self-esteem shouldn't be wrapped up in a device designed to deliver other people's to-do lists?'

Don't keep all your eggs in one basket...

...In case you drop the basket and break them all. If our only window on the world is our BlackBerry, then we're exposed. When even the best technologies in the world have their difficulties, it's clear that you need a back-up plan. But it needs to be identified before the event not when you're whining that your world is falling around you because your BlackBerry has run out of battery. It needn't involve yet more technology – a pen and paper is pretty good, so is a slim notebook with all your phone numbers. When things go wrong, learn from them so they don't catch you out again. Think of Confucious' words: *the wise man learns when he can, the fool learns when he has to*. Flat batteries and other assorted hiccups are usually telling us something, maybe that it's time to do more by phone? Don't fight such scenarios, as guess what? If you don't learn, it tends to happen all over again!

A good look?

Picture yourself in a crowded departure lounge at Gatwick at 8:00am. You peer into the palm of your hand, looking for the important email that Sir Charles wants you to read. No signal! You snort, you swear out loud, you adjust your laptop bag and, for a moment, you look around as if waiting for Mum to tell you what to do next. Picture how that looks to others. Ask yourself: *is it a good look*? Do you appear to be in control, or do you look like life is just happening to you? Now swap that for a picture of someone taking everything in their stride and going with the flow. Isn't that a better look? Do you think George Clooney would still be cast as the romantic lead if he looked like the sort of chap who checks his phone every ten minutes to see if she's called yet?

Blackberry Smoothie

The Blackberry Smoothie is the type of guy who peppers his conversation with phrases like '120% effort'. You only see what he means once you realise you're getting 20% of his attention, with the other 100% going to his BlackBerry. We're all familiar with his predecessor, the shoulder-surfer, the sort who glances over your shoulder to look for someone more interesting to talk to, but at least they were looking for *people*. The *Blackberry Smoothie* is merely on the lookout for more mails, for little icons of people. Jean Baudrilliard once said that executives were like joggers: stop a jogger and they will continue to run on the spot while they talk; some executives will carry on cutting deals and pawing the ground long after business is over for the day. Sure enough, it's now all too normal to see people socialising while simultaneously checking their BlackBerry. Does no-one care to be charming anymore?

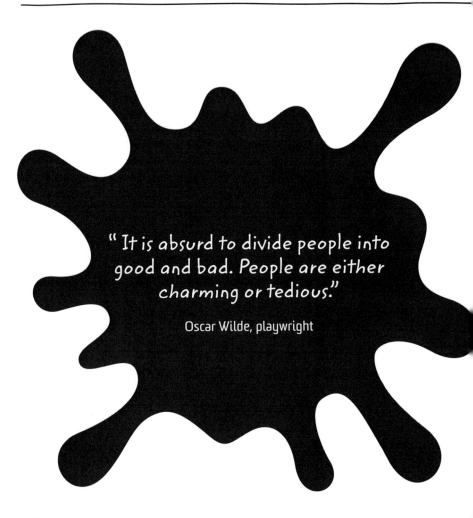

" It is absurd to divide people into good and bad. People are either charming or tedious."

Oscar Wilde, playwright

The eyes have it

Many of the friends and enemies of former US president Bill Clinton have commented on the man's extraordinary degree of charm, especially in one-to-one conversation. Hard-bitten Washington journalists and politician's wives alike have breathlessly observed Clinton's ability to make a person *feel like they were the only person in the room*. In Clinton's case the room is likely to be full of bigwigs, so it's no small skill. Who can say how Clinton does it? Charm is an ineffable, mysterious thing, but it probably starts in the eyes.

Eyes are for conversation, conversations are for relationships, and relationships are the stuff of life. By contrast, our hands are for tools. Tools are for tasks, and tasks are what you do at work. If you're looking at something in your hand while you're talking, then you are at work – it's no longer a social event, at least not for the luckless person who's stuck with you. Even if you only peek for an instant, you will break the spell of whatever charm you have.

Obviously Bill would be less charming if he were to glance up and down from a Rubik's Cube while he chatted, but if that's so obvious why do so many people still need to be told to put their BlackBerry away?

Don't take it to places where you don't really need it

Tip 2

Parties, for example (even office parties) must surely be a BlackBerry-free zone. This rule is much easier to obey once you recall how it feels when you're talking to someone at a party and they...*take out their phone and turn their attention to it.* It feels insulting and it looks incredibly rude, not to mention a wee bit juvenile. Take your BlackBerry to the office party and you'll increase your chances of getting the damn thing out, and thereby winning the rude and juvenile rosette for yourself. We reach for our phones so reflexively that it's easy to forget that it amounts to a mild snub for the person we're talking to. In any case, if you know how to have a good time at a party – and who wouldn't want *that* description in their obituary – then you should naturally forget about your BlackBerry. And that's when you forget you left it in the toilet, the bar, the cab, or in the hands of a thief. No configuration of office equipment has ever got the party started, not even the photocopier (despite often taking a starring role later on in the evening...).

Less job title and more leadership

Do you recall this sort of telling-off from your childhood?

> Parent: 'Are you going to do as you're told?'
> You: 'Why should I?'
> Parent: 'Because *I* say so!'

Your six-year-old self wasn't persuaded by the old '…because I say so' routine and nor are your co-workers – so stop using your job title to get them to do what you want. Sure, people will usually do what their line manager tells them to do, and they do it solely because it's the line manager who said so, but is that true loyalty? Aren't they just acting out of fear of the hierarchy, rather than respect? Best results come when your team follow you because of what you know, what you do and the sort of person you are.

Most of us are rightly suspicious of anyone who is quick to introduce themselves as the Acting Assistant Vice President of Administrative Development. It's not hard to make up a slick job title. A job title is not enough. Dishing out non-stop instructions on your BlackBerry is not enough. 'We are what we commonly do' – so said Aristotle, a man who has inspired countless followers over thousands of years without ever having been, as far as anyone can tell, anyone's line manager.

We're sorry to interrupt your regular programming

Inevitably there will be times when you just can't avoid an important call from work coming in just when you've sat down to a nice restaurant dinner with friends. But do you really need to answer it? There can be no winners if you do. If it's a truly important matter the caller will be embarrassed or annoyed that you took the call during a social occasion, your companions will be miffed that you've made them second best. If you run outside to take the call on the pavement, you'll risk becoming one of those rude folk who see nothing wrong in scorching through restaurant doors and knocking down pedestrians simply to bellow '...can you hear me now?' So there is really only one thing to do, and it also happens to be the cool thing to do. Without averting your eyes from your dinner companions, take out your nagging phone, switch it off and then replace it in your pocket with no further comment. There – you've just paid a small but artful compliment to your guests, and taken on an air of mystery at the same time. That's got to look more impressive than having your leash yanked by an unseen hand.

No-one wants to see it

Tip 5

At some point in our recent history it has become semi-acceptable to leave our phones out when in social settings. We leave them out on the table, on the kitchen worktop, in the conference room, at the bar, you name it. How odd that a small design feature – the phone is designed to interrupt you, and you're supposed to keep an eye out for that – has mutated into a social norm with grim consequences. If the phone were to be designed from scratch today it's not inconceivable that some of the more niche models would go on sale without a ringing bell. After all, the Victorians made sure that the first few phones were palmed off into the servant quarters. No-one would have felt the need to answer it just because it was ringing. His Lordship would have thought it a bally terrible affair if he were forced to put down his copy of *The Times* and rise from his chair every time some jack-a-nape sought to interrupt him with some balderdash about a horse and carriage parked with its gas-lamps still on.

To leave your BlackBerry on the table at dinner is to put your dining companions on notice that, with the mere ring of a bell, they might be demoted in favour of callers unknown. It's like a dinner where everybody is forced to watch the host play a game of *Buckaroo* all night.

Come on. Put it away. No-one wants to see it.

Blackberry Crumble

A *Blackberry Crumble* is the moment of despair experienced by the *Fool* in the close-to-catastrophic event of discovering that they've lost their beloved device. The *Crumble* is first experienced as a nagging feeling of lightness followed by an uncontrollable patting movement to the chest and buttocks. The frantic patting is usually limited to the *Fool's* chest and buttocks only, but paranoia is a common symptom and so bystanders are advised to retreat to a safe distance. A full-blown, final-stage *Crumble* is characterised by gloom, aggression and a humiliating round of fishing between the ankles of everyone in the bar, a search which may be carried out several times and with no explanation or humour. If you think that your drinking companion is a *Fool* undergoing a *Blackberry Crumble* then the most you can do for them is to clear the area of tables and chairs and let them get on with it.

"The superior man, ...when in a state of security does not forget the possibility of ruin. When all is orderly, he does not forget that disorder may come. Thus his person is not endangered, and his States and all their clans are preserved."

Confucius (551 BC - 479 BC)

Do the basics right now

Tip 1

What would happen if you lost this useful device? Or if it were stolen? Would you still be able to perform at the conference you have flown half-way around the world for? Would you still be able to function – would you be able to call the office or your partner's mobile? Record your five essential mobile numbers (that's usually all you really need) in the back of a note book, pin them to the corner of the kitchen cork-board, or if you want to be like Madonna, have them tattooed on the inside of your thigh.

Get someone to show how your passwords and your filters and your folders all fit together, and then write it down. Copy your SIM cards and purchase a cheap phone for backup. If you drop your back-up phone into your drink during a night on the tiles you'll only lose your dignity and maybe even keep your drink, depending on how much you paid for it and whether anyone saw the phone kerplunk into your glass. What you won't lose is your emails and years of contacts.

Have a policy about policies

If you don't want to fork out for insurance, write off your BlackBerry from day one. Go on. Take it out of the box, stare it in the face, say your goodbyes and make your peace with your loss. And when that day comes, that day when you look down onto the restaurant table and see only a sickening void where your darling BlackBerry should be, take it like a man – make no mention of the insurance you had every opportunity to buy. While you're at it, men, you should accept that men lose stuff more than women do. A quick survey of the world's lost property collections will reveal that men lose far more possessions than women, even though the average woman never leaves the house without a vast arsenal of widgets, gubbins, baubles, gewjaws and doodads. Happily, men can be scatty and still make a huge contribution to the world: Einstein could figure out almost anything and yet, judging by his appearance in photos, finding his comb in the morning was a gigantic intellectual challenge.

Make a friend of bureaucracy and indifference

Tip 3

If you've ever attended a police station in a *Blackberry Crumble* moment to report your phone as lost or stolen, you'll have some idea of what it must be like to be prosecuted for wasting police time. The desk sergeant will not be happy: he has to record the whole sorry episode in sub-atomic detail. It's best not to act like some crime has taken place, or that you've been inconvenienced, because however bad you feel about it you can be sure the policeman is even more fed up. Out comes his biro, down go his shoulders and suddenly you're recounting your sad story to the top of his greying head. If you don't see his face again until it's time for you to leave, it's because he doesn't care. He *can't* care: he has more important things to do. He thought he was joining the force to protect old ladies and lock up bad guys: you thought a BlackBerry would save you time. The two of you together make for a sad kitchen-sink drama in which none of the characters get what they want. And when it comes to the moment when the policeman asks what sort of phone has been lost, try not to announce the model number of your BlackBerry like you'd announce ownership of a Van Gogh. Not unless you want the policeman to file his copy of your paperwork next to an open window.

Observe radio silence

Tip 4

Chirpy types love to say, 'If God gives you lemons, make lemonade!' They do have a point. And when you lose your phone, God not only gives you some lemons but also a bottle of gin and a frosted glass filled with tonic water and ice, nicely arranged with today's papers and the TV remote. Now, what do you think God hopes you'll make with all that? Almost certainly, God wants you to make a long, cool drink to go with an evening of blessed peace and quiet. The chances are you're not missing anything important. You should observe the good things that come from your radio silence. The chances are that tonight, without your phone, your thoughts are going to be that little bit more clear. You'll be that little bit more free to do something you might not have done had you been glued to the yammering BlackBerry. It's up to you to make the most of it. Bottoms up.

Maybe you've not faced up to your habit

Tip 5

If you've identified yourself as being on par with rats and gamblers, then good. Next stage is to recognise you might need a little help getting over it. Alcoholics are always thinking about their next drink, *Blackberry Fools* are usually thinking about their next 'twitch'. And just like alcoholics, they'll find excuses…

'I just need to pop out to the car for a moment.'

… they'll rationalise…

'If I don't I wont get a bonus.'

…and they'll create their own universe

'Everybody works this way now.'

So, recognise you might be an addict. It's up to you whether you want to take that analogy any further – going cold turkey, swearing to a life of abstinence etc – but certainly, the analogy's a good start. Putting down the BlackBerry gets easier once you look at it from the addict's point of view.

Blackberry Jam

A *Blackberry Jam* is what a *Fool* risks getting into if they hope to run their entire life through the screen of a BlackBerry. It's impractical and they end up in a serious *Jam*. Technology companies will Tell Us What We Want to Hear, and what we want to hear is that they've finally made a gadget that takes away the pain of modern life, available now and in a range of natty colours. It's not the tech company's fault. They're only working with what they've been given: a generation which expects too much. We're spoiled by having more computer power in our kitchens than NASA needed to put man on the moon. If our fridges are almost capable of time travel, our phones should be able to solve all our problems, especially our addictive behaviour, yes?

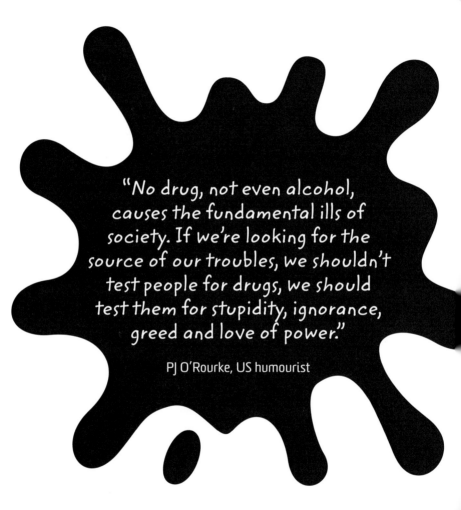

"No drug, not even alcohol, causes the fundamental ills of society. If we're looking for the source of our troubles, we shouldn't test people for drugs, we should test them for stupidity, ignorance, greed and love of power."

PJ O'Rourke, US humourist

Count to six

Tip 1

There are at least six things that go into a well-rounded life; relationships, career, health, money, fun and your contribution to others. If you stare at all six through the screen of your BlackBerry you'll encounter a problem familiar to those who don't wash their saucepans properly: the taste of last night's garlic in this morning's porridge. It's a shame to glimpse tomorrow's parties through a grey mist of spreadsheets and deadlines. Remember that a BlackBerry exists to serve the needs of the workplace *first*, well ahead of everything else that makes up the good life. Sure, you can use your BlackBerry calendar to remind you that you need to call the kids to say goodnight, re-do your CV, jog round the company car park, ask your boss for a raise or sponsor your colleague's charity bike ride, but there's a bit of a work flavour to all of those things, no? Why do you think that is?

Know what's really important to you

Tip 2

It's a sad fact, but we often realise that our health and our relationships are important only once we lose them. It follows that you should actively affirm what is and isn't important to you. If something is important you will give it time. If you're not giving it time, you are saying it is not important – mind who sees *that*. Recognise that life might not be better tomorrow or next week or 'after this project': it can instead be absolutely perfect now, if you allow yourself to enjoy it and be in the moment. In a heavily time-driven world, especially the hard-facing commercial world, the pursuit of success can exclude all the things that really do make us successful, not to mention spoil our enjoyment of the journey.

Switch off

Tip 3

Work used to come with natural endings: 5pm, the weekend, the factory's two-week summer shutdown. Now we must consciously choose when our working day ends. It's hard, but if we don't force ourselves to clock off then the working day never ends, at which point our health suffers, our friends lose touch, we grow humourless at home, we shelve our entrepreneurial dreams and we grow indifferent to the welfare of others. After all, we've had a heck of a day in the office. Keep the evening clear of work and emails several hours before sleep, otherwise anxiety will be carried over to the bedroom. *Relax.* Try planning to do nothing.

Muck out your silos

A BlackBerry world can send people deep into their silos. Every relationship needs a bit of maintenance work now and again, and for that you need people together in the room, not on the end of a phone. Without enough person-to-person contact, with too much reliance on email, small differences of opinion can grow into huge gulfs between us and our fellow workers and friends. A missed chance to meet up can grow into falling out or losing touch altogether, at home and at work. It's because email cannot really convey the emotions and nuances of whatever might be causing the problem. It's not unknown for some forward thinking companies to have sessions or allotted days where email is banned. You can bet that those are the days people talk about the opportunities rather than the challenges: how they can support each other rather than scramble to find who's fault it is. It's marvellous what will happen once the distractions of technology are out of the way.

Use batch processing

You *can* check your BlackBerry every few minutes, but why do you want to? All you're doing is constantly interrupting your ability to concentrate on the true task in hand – which is presumably not just responding to mail. It's becoming clear that interruptions have an effect upon the human brain that last longer than the duration of the interruption itself: some studies suggest that your focus only returns fully one minute after the end of the typical interruption, even for just for something simple and quick like taking time out to check email. You can end up in a *Blackberry Jam*. It follows that we need to get email back to where it should be: a tool to be used in context. You can get there by batching your processing, by checking more mails on fewer occasions. The world really will not fall apart in between each serving of peanut.

Blackberry Tart

Blackberry Tart is the bitter-sweet feeling that the more one uses a BlackBerry, the less productive one becomes. It's easy to see why. When we walk into a noisy cocktail party we must raise our voices, and everyone else must raise their voices in response, and so on until everyone tires of the din and leaves. The BlackBerry has the same effect. Anyone with a BlackBerry can add their two cents to an email conversation, day or night, from anywhere. The result is one big shouty cocktail party held in a ballroom large enough to host everyone in the online world (pop. 4 billion). The tart truth about the BlackBerry is that *in a networked world there can be no such thing as a labour-saving device.* If your BlackBerry gives you the power to send an extra 50 emails a day then you'd better hope and pray that no-one else has one too.

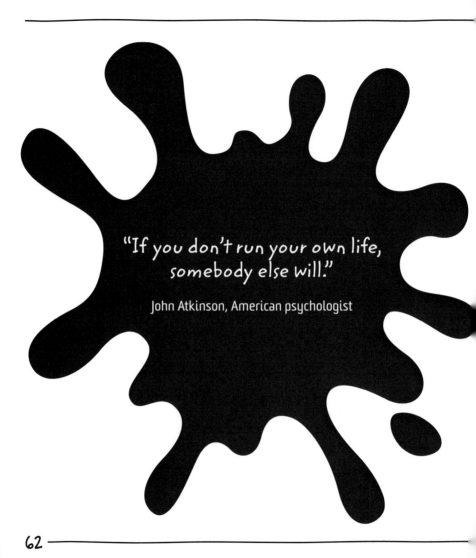

"If you don't run your own life,
somebody else will."

John Atkinson, American psychologist

Dear Reader, I harried him

Tip 1   When writing to a colleague, you should do your best to....

....collate all of your...

...information/requests into one mail...

...rather than just off-loading single thoughts onto your....

...unlucky recipient...

...who is forced to sit there and tot it up...

... like some satanic itemised bill.

Send fewer mails and make 'em short

Remember those pictures of nuclear chain reactions in your science book at school? Email is very similar: every one you send seems to proliferate a couple more. Once you start using cc or long mailing lists you're risking an uncontrollable chain reaction, so for everybody's safety it's time to review those mailing lists. Pay particular attention to your use of cc. When you send an email 'To' some people but only 'cc' others, effectively you're saying: 'Some of you need to hear my news more than others', a strange distinction when everyone gets your news at the same time. Don't forget that there's beauty in brevity. Take Shakespeare's famous phrase: "*To be or not to be*?", despite being the best-known sentence in English literature, and despite referring to the biggest and most profound question of them all – is life worth all the aggro? – Shakespeare's phrase uses no words longer than one syllable. You can cover a lot of ground in six syllables, so the next time you find yourself bashing away on the keyboard late at night, consider whether you need to be married to every one of the 10,000 words in your monthly sales report. If you're still unconvinced, consider George Orwell's famous line: "*The enemy of clear language is insincerity.*" In other words, if your emails are lengthy and full of mealy-mouthed jargon it's probably because you don't really mean what you're saying. Speak your mind if you want to go home on time.

Remember that email wars are like real wars

Real wars are easy to start but hard to finish. Likewise, anyone caught up in an email war needs superhuman self-control not to launch the last word, and that's why such wars drag on. Think hard before *you* join the fighting. Remember that much email responding is simply fire-fighting. If you take a step back and look for the deeper issues underneath the surface issues then you're more likely to come up with an intelligent and creative solution. If that doesn't work, your IT dept might half-seriously consider the same solution that US stand-up comic Chris Rock proposed for America's gun control problem: make every bullet cost $5,000. "That way", Rock said, "*if you heard about someone getting shot, you'd **know** they probably deserved it*". Too bad no-one has taken this reasoning to our emails. Let's look forward to the day when BlackBerry users are not permitted to write more than ten emails a week. That way, if you heard about someone receiving a snotty email you'd know they probably deserved it. It's true that email-capping would probably make it harder to locate the owner of the rotting cheese left to ferment in the office fridge, but what price peace?

Break the pattern

Tip 4

A pattern is a way of working. Notice any patterns with your BlackBerry? Do you leave it by the bed and on your desk at work? Is it out of the question that you'd ever turn off the ringer and just check voicemail once a day instead? Do you really need to keep buying accessories for it? Is leaving the house with the battery only half-charged your idea of Alfred Hitchcock-style tension? Do you sometimes catch yourself thinking about trading it in for a newer model only a week after you last did so? Must you really check messages at the dentist? In the car? In the arms of a loved one? During an out-of body experience? Think of all the things you used to do before that tart taste of 'I've got to work' feeling kicked in. Truly, you don't need to have it blink at you all the time. Notice these compulsive patterns of behaviour and resolve to break them before they break you. If you can't break the addiction, consider a cross-addiction instead: buy a Tamagotchi – it'll nag you until the end of time and doesn't come with a monthly bill.

Fewer excuses and *more accountability*.

True leadership is where we take ownership. We give clear instructions, preferably verbal instructions and not via a garbled email. If we need to say sorry for something we've done, we say it to someone's face so they can hear in our voice that we really mean it.

Email has a notoriously deadening effect on our words. That's been particularly true of emailed apologies ever since the word 'sorry' joined the list of doubled-edged phrases. You know what a double-edged phrase is: any phrase that seems friendly enough in print but, in real-life, often conceals a raging sea of hostility. Examples of double-edged phrases include:

> 'Sir'
> 'Madam'
> 'With the greatest respect'
> 'I hear what you're saying'
> 'Welcome to my world'

I'm so *sorry* that's what's happened to the word 'sorry', *Madam*.

Conclusion

We know your BlackBerry's never going to go away.
Technology and work have always gone hand in hand. Technology
has always had an upside and a downside, and it's always been
unstoppable. And just because it can be used to improve working
life doesn't mean that we have to like it, or be a slave to it, or make
a fetish of it. After all, history is full of folk who stood firm against
what they believed to be the wrong kind of progress on the line. Look
at the Luddites, who smashed up the looms of the cotton industry
and wrecked havoc during the Industrial Revolution.

But who wants to be a Luddite?

History has not been kind to them. Their name is synonymous with stick-in-the-muds who rage against the popular notion of progress. Our corporate leaders have decided BlackBerrys makes sense, and that's that. In any case, there will always be the next new thing that comes along and upends how we, the workers, go about our daily business.

We know the BlackBerry's not all bad.
We can see the huge value it brings to our working lives.
The ability to maintain a continuous and mobile link with
the office was unheard of ten or so years ago. Many of us
wonder how on earth we managed without it. The same
is true of most other gizmos like sat-nav and laptops.
Technology is woven into the fabric of life, of which the
BlackBerry is just one part.

Too bad it doesn't take long for us to become totally dependent upon new technology. Over time we become less able to survive without it. We lose our initiative, just like those sat-nav owners who cause no end of problems by allowing their screens to lead them on ridiculous routes to impossible places. Just as few of us seem capable of reading a map these days, fewer of us seem able to deal with a situation where we can't use our BlackBerry.

Technology and especially that which can be considered mobile (the Smartphone, the laptop, iPhone, etc.) also creates what is euphemistically known as *jobspill*. This is where your working time extends increasingly into your leisure, personal and family time. You see it everywhere, on trains, on planes and (where it is not illegal) in automobiles. The executive with their eyes glued to their laptop, their thumb scrolling up and down their BlackBerry, or the phone stuck to their ear is a very common sight: it seems these days that everyone is permanently on call. But as we have seen throughout this book, there is always a choice to not be on call all of the time.

So how should we live with our BlackBerrys?

Turn it off at the end of the day. Don't be tempted to keep it on your bedside table at night. There are more important things to do in the bedroom.

●

Don't take it away with you on family days out or on holiday, otherwise you will never really leave the office. Even while you watch the sun go down in Bermuda, Dave from accounts will sort of be there with you, your wife's hand in your hand…ahh, just the three of you, together at last.

●

Don't become a slave to your BlackBerry's buzz. Turn off the notification alarms before you end up with attention deficit disorder.

●

Do remember that face-to-face communcation is best, followed by phone calls. Email is a very distant third.

When out with your friends, look into their eyes – not your palm or your lap, otherwise it won't be long before you're sitting alone.

●

Establish a Plan B for those instances where you might not have your BlackBerry to hand. Learn to use a pen and paper again. If nothing else, the handwriting practice might spell the end of your Christmas cards resembling a ransom notes from a festive serial killer.

●

Remember there are always choices: you just need to become conscious of exercising them.

●

If all else fails, enrol yourself onto one of the many 12-step addiction programmes: true enlightenment will await you at the end of it.

Let's finish on an intriguing question. Imagine you're holding two pigeons, one in each hand. The pigeon in your left hand is alive, the pigeon in your right hand is dead. Now imagine throwing both pigeons up into the air at the same time. Where do you think each will pigeon land?

•

You can use the laws of physics to work out where the dead pigeon will land – the weight of bird, the launch angle, wind conditions, that sort of thing – but there's no way of knowing where our live pigeon is off to. The live pigeon is *autonomous*. It will land wherever it chooses: maybe Nelson's Column, maybe Big Ben, maybe off to the country to land in a nice blackberry bush for some lunch and a spot of people watching. Like Richard Branson, the live pigeon will do whatever takes its fancy. In so doing, the bird shows us that autonomy – the freedom to make our own choices – must be part of what it means to really be alive.

•

As addictive as your BlackBerry is, it's important to believe that you really do have autonomy over it.

•

Otherwise, which one of our two pigeons are you?

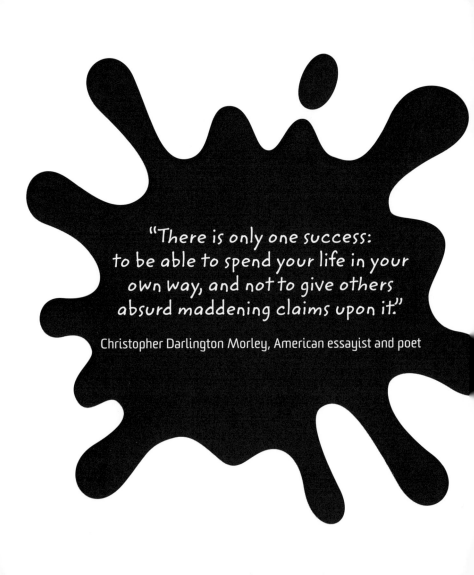

"There is only one success:
to be able to spend your life in your
own way, and not to give others
absurd maddening claims upon it."

Christopher Darlington Morley, American essayist and poet

Registered office

Capstone Publishing Ltd. (A Wiley Company), The Atrium, Southern Gate, Chichester, West Sussex, PO19 8SQ, United Kingdom

For details of our global editorial offices, for customer services and for information about how to apply for permission to reuse the copyright material in this book please see our website at www.wiley.com.

Library of Congress Cataloguing-in-Publication Data to come

ISBN: 9781906465667

A catalogue record for this book is available from the British Library.

Set in Sommet Regular by Mackerel Limited

Printed in Great Britain by TJ International Ltd. Padstow